ANTIPASTO

ITALIAN STARTERS, SOUPS AND SNACKS

Angus&Robertson
An imprint of HarperCollins*Publishers*

An Angus & Robertson Publication
Angus&Robertson, an imprint of
HarperCollins Publishers
25 Ryde Road, Pymble, Sydney NSW 2073, Australia
31 View Road, Glenfield, Auckland 10, New Zealand
77–85 Fulham Palace Road, London W6 8JB, United Kingdom
10 East 53rd Street, New York NY 10022, USA
First published in Australia in 1994

National Library of Australia
Cataloguing-in-Publication data:
Antipasto: Italian starters, soups and snacks.
ISBN 0207 18604 9.
1. Appetisers. 2. Cookery, Italian.
641.812

Additional text by Pamela Allardice
Design by Liz Seymour
Illustrations by Penny Lovelock
Photography by Rowan Fotheringham
Food Styling by Donna Hay and Beth Pittman
Printed in Hong Kong

9 8 7 6 5 4 3 2 1
97 96 95 94

CONTENTS

Introduction 5

Breads

Soups and Salads

Pasta

Light Meals

Index 56

INTRODUCTION

**ITALIANS ARE GREAT LOVERS OF ANTIPASTO
(MEANING, LITERALLY, 'BEFORE THE MEAL') — THOSE
TEMPTING MORSELS BEAUTIFULLY AND COLOURFULLY
ARRANGED ON LARGE PLATTERS TO STIMULATE
THE DINER'S APPETITE.**

I n recent times, antipasto has come to refer not only to a traditional 'appetiser' course, but also to a whole new way of eating where a great selection of small and appealing foods are offered at once. An antipasto plate can therefore be the basis of an extravagant buffet or a picnic in the country, or a meal on its own.

You can prepare good antipasto from traditional recipes or simply buy a selection of fresh ingredients from the delicatessen, vegetable market or fish shop on the way home. In fact, it is the freshness of the ingredients and the ease of preparation which characterise antipasto dishes. Few of the recipes require more than minimal cooking. You can be endlessly creative, experimenting with inventive fillings like sun-dried tomatoes, pesto and green herb sauces, and delectable savoury morsels such as olives, red chilli peppers, garden-fresh vegetables and marinated dishes such as baby artichokes and carrots in lemon vinegar.

Buon appetito!

BREADS

BREAD, IN MANY FORMS, IS AN IMPORTANT ELEMENT IN THE ITALIAN DIET, ESPECIALLY IN APPETISERS. EACH REGION HAS ITS SPECIAL BREADS AND THE RANGE OF SIZES AND SHAPES IS FASCINATING.

Try thin, crisp sheets of *carta di musica*, from Sardinia, so-called because of the crackling noise it makes when broken, or pita bread, wrapped around a variety of fillings in the Greek style, from Calabria, or *grissini*, Turin's re-nowned breadsticks, or fabulous *focaccia* filled with all kinds of marvels. *Panini* are delicious Italian-style sandwiches. The Tuscans sometimes use bread as the basis for a thick and hearty soup. Then there is *bruschetta*, usually a thick slice of country-style bread that has been grilled and rubbed with garlic and oil, and can serve as the beginning for all manner of toppings — capsicum, eggplant, artichokes, avocado and strong-flavoured cheeses.

In Italy, the different breads are often served in cafés and bars, and are likely to be eaten while standing at a counter. Bread and bread-based dishes are seen as being more of a snack or even a casual meal in their own right, rather than just as an accessory to a meal.

Bruschetta with Caviale di Funghi

4 slices crusty bread, cut 1 cm (½ in) thick
2 cloves garlic, cut in half and with the green centre stem removed
extra virgin olive oil (about 4 tablespoons)
salt and freshly ground black pepper

1 Toast bread slices on both sides under a grill, or even better, over an open fire. While still hot rub one side of each slice with half a clove of garlic. Rub it in well, until most of the clove is used up. Drizzle about 1 tablespoon of oil over each slice and salt and pepper liberally. Serve hot.

Serves 4

Caviale di Funghi

This mushroom and pine nut 'caviar' makes an excellent topping for bruschetta *or it can be used as a dip.*

250 g (8 oz) mushrooms of choice
60 g (2 oz) butter
4 spring onions, finely chopped
1 clove garlic, minced
1 tablespoon dry white wine
2 tablespoons toasted pine nuts
1 tablespoon finely chopped fresh parsley
1 to 2 tablespoons sour cream

1 Chop mushrooms to give a fine but slightly chunky texture.
2 Melt butter in a frying pan and gently sauté mushrooms and spring onions for 5 minutes. Add garlic and wine and sauté 2 to 3 minutes more, or until mixture is dry. Remove from heat, cool, then stir in pine nuts and parsley. Moisten with enough sour cream to give a texture which will not break up, but which is not runny.

Serves 4

MORE ON BRUSCHETTA

Called *fettunta* or *fregolotta* in Tuscany, *bruschetta* is old, traditional food which has been around for centuries. It was eaten by shepherds and farm workers on its own, or used as a base for a snack with a more substantial topping.

VERSATILE CARROTS

Bright orange carrots, with their crisp, juicy texture and sweet flavour may be easily grown in the vegetable patch. Their pretty feathery tops mean they do not look out of place in a flower bed, or even in window boxes, either. If you grow your own carrots, be sure to utilise these pretty tops as garnishes on an antipasto platter.

There are a great number of carrot varieties available. Most common ones are long and slender, and these are best for use raw or, as here, lightly cooked and marinated, for they tend to have the best flavour. Avoid too-small and immature carrots as they will not have had a chance to develop their sweetness. Older, larger carrots are usually best suited for casseroles and stews, having a hard core and a slightly bitter flavour.

These marinated carrot sticks make a good addition to an antipasto spread, giving colour, texture and that touch of 'heat' with the chilli. They are also delicious served with a barbeque or taken on a picnic as they are ideal finger food. More or less chilli may be used, to taste, and you could experiment with other herbs than the basil. Carrots treated this way last for weeks if kept covered in the refrigerator.

Sfogliatine

Sfogliatine ripiene *(literally, stuffed pastries)* are small, filled pastries made of flaky or puff pastry. The original comes from Liguria and has a cheese and spinach stuffing, but many different fillings are successful, such as the tomato, olive and mozzarella used here. Sfogliatine can be made smaller and served as finger food to nibble on with drinks.

1 large tomato
125 g (4 oz) fresh mozzarella, cut into very small cubes
¼ teaspoon finely chopped fresh basil
¼ teaspoon finely chopped fresh oregano, or a pinch of dried
8 to 10 black olives, pitted and sliced
salt and freshly ground black pepper
220 g (7 oz) puff pastry
1 large egg, beaten

1 Preheat oven to 190°C (375°F).
2 Dip tomato into boiling water for a few seconds, then peel, seed and chop into very small cubes. Combine with mozzarella, basil, oregano and olives, then season with salt and pepper.
3 On a floured surface, roll out pastry to 2 to 3 mm (⅛ in) thickness. Cut out circles of 10 cm (4 in) diameter, and paint around the rims of each with egg. Place some filling on one half of each circle, fold over the other side to encase it, and press tightly to seal. Trim around the outer edges with a crinkle-cutter, or press with the tines of a fork. Brush the tops with remaining egg, and transfer to an ungreased baking tray.
4 Bake for 15 to 20 minutes, or until golden and puffed. Serve hot or cold, as a snack.

Makes about 15, or 24 smaller versions for finger food.

Serves 4

Marinated Carrots

1½ teaspoons salt
8 carrots, cut into sticks
2 tablespoons olive oil
3 cloves garlic, cut into halves
¼ teaspoon chilli flakes
1 tablespoon finely chopped fresh basil
white wine vinegar

1 Bring a large saucepan of water to the boil, add 1 teaspoon salt and carrot sticks. Boil until just cooked but still crisp, approximately 3 to 4 minutes. Drain and cool slightly before transferring to a bowl.
2 Add remaining ½ teaspoon salt, olive oil, garlic, chilli flakes and basil. Add enough vinegar to just cover carrots, then toss to distribute ingredients.
3 Cover and refrigerate for at least 24 hours before use. Drain before serving.

Serves 4

Grilled Polenta with Gorgonzola and Walnuts

These little bite-sized treats make great finger food, or they can be made on a bigger scale and served individually as a starter. To clean the polenta saucepan, simply fill it with cold water and leave overnight; the crust will soak off and fall away.

POLENTA
7 cups (1¾ litres/56 fl oz) water
2⅔ cups (350 g/11 oz) polenta (cornmeal)
30 g (1 oz) butter

TOPPING
75 g (2½ oz) butter, softened
1 cup (100 g/3½ oz) walnut pieces, finely chopped
200 g (6½ oz) Gorgonzola cheese, or other creamy blue vein
2 tablespoons brandy
freshly ground black pepper

1 To prepare polenta: Bring water to the boil in a large heavy-based saucepan. Reduce to a simmer, then gradually pour in polenta, stirring constantly. Keep stirring until the polenta lifts away from the sides of the pan, about 20 minutes. Stir in butter. Turn out into an oiled pan to 1 cm thickness and smooth surface of mixture. Leave to cool and set.
2 To prepare topping: Blend butter, walnuts, Gorgonzola and brandy together in a bowl. Season with a few good grinds of black pepper.
3 Turn on grill to high heat.
4 With a 4 cm (1½ in) cookie cutter, cut out circles from the polenta. Place under grill and toast on one side. Turn over and place a good spoonful of topping on each one, then return to grill. Serve as soon as the cheese is bubbling and the walnuts slightly toasted.

Serves 4

WALNUTS

Walnuts and rich cheese sounds exotic — and these flavours do manage to come together in a rich, mellow and somehow undeniably Italian way. The walnuts bring a slight sweetness to this dish, too. It is an elegant antipasto offering to serve to guests, with the flavours and textures making it especially appealing and intriguing.

Borlotti Bean Dip

Reminiscent of the Arab hummus, this dip is based on la capriata, the broad bean purée found in various forms in all the southern regions of Italy. Any type of dried bean can be substituted, and if dried broad beans can be found, all the better. Use 185 g (6 oz) dried beans if starting from scratch.

1 clove garlic
1 tablespoon fresh rosemary leaves
400 g (13 oz) canned borlotti beans, drained and rinsed
1 teaspoon tomato paste
½ teaspoon salt
2 tablespoons fresh lemon juice
3 tablespoons extra virgin olive oil
chilli paste or sauce, to taste
extra rosemary sprigs, to garnish

1 Finely chop garlic and rosemary together. Blend in a food processor or mince finely with a fork with beans, tomato paste and salt until a smooth purée forms.
2 Add lemon juice, olive oil and a little chilli paste. Process to blend, then taste. Add more chilli, if preferred.
3 Refrigerate, covered, until ready to use; this dip is even more delicious if left for 24 hours.

Serve as a dip, or on triangles of plain toast, topped with rosemary.

Gorgonzola Sticks

1¼ cups (155 g/5 oz) plain (all-purpose) flour
pinch salt
¼ teaspoon paprika
cold water
60 g (2 oz) butter
60 g (2 oz) Gorgonzola cheese, or other blue vein

1 Preheat oven to 200°C (400°F) and grease a baking tray.
2 This step may be done in a food processor. Sieve flour and salt into a bowl and stir in paprika. Rub butter in well, then add cold water, a little at a time, to form a stiff dough. Knead lightly.
3 Roll out on a floured surface to a rectangle of about 3 mm (⅛ in) thick. Crumble or grate cheese evenly over half the dough. Fold over the other half to completely cover cheese.
4 Roll again over the top until quite thin and the cheese just begins to show through pastry. Trim edges with a sharp knife, then cut pastry into sticks of about 5 mm (¼ in) wide and 8 cm (3 in) long. Transfer to prepared baking tray and bake in the oven until lightly browned, about 10 minutes.

Makes about 50 sticks

Onion Focaccia

Using a dough which is yeastless but with a good flavour and texture, this focaccia is quick and easy. The filling, which can be made in advance and stored in the refrigerator, can also be used to stuff a bought plain focaccia.

DOUGH

4 cups (500 g/1 lb) plain (all-purpose) flour, sifted

3 tablespoons caster sugar

1 teaspoon salt

2 eggs, lightly beaten

¾ cup (180 ml/6 fl oz) olive oil

⅓ cup (100 ml/3 fl oz) dry white wine

FILLING

3 tablespoons olive oil

850 g (1¾ lb) onions, sliced and then chopped

3 tablespoons dry white wine

salt and freshly ground black pepper

2¾ cups (700 ml/23 fl oz) water

6 black olives, pitted and sliced

2 teaspoons tiny capers

FOR THE TOP

olive oil

coarse sea salt

cayenne pepper

1 To prepare dough: Mix flour, sugar and salt in a bowl. Gradually incorporate eggs, oil and wine, beating well after each addition.

A little more wine or flour may be needed to form a loose dough. Transfer to a floured board and knead 2 to 3 minutes, or until smooth. (This whole step can be done in a food processor.) Cover and refrigerate for at least 30 minutes.

2 Preheat oven to 200°C (400°F). Grease a large rectangular scone tray and toss it with flour.

3 To prepare filling: Heat oil in a large, heavy saucepan. Add onions and wine, and salt and pepper well. Simmer, uncovered, for 5 minutes, stirring from time to time. Add water. Simmer until all the liquid has evaporated; the mixture must be quite dry. Stir in olives and capers.

4 Roll out dough on a lightly floured board to a rectangle about 1 cm (½ in) thick. Spread filling over one end to cover half, leaving a rim of 2 to 3 cm (1 in) free. Fold over other half to encase, and lightly press edges together. Transfer to prepared tray, drizzle over 1 to 2 tablespoons of olive oil and sprinkle with salt and cayenne. Dimple surface using fingertips.

5 Transfer to the oven and bake until golden and cooked through, 20 to 25 minutes. Cool slightly before removing from tray. Can be served warm or at room temperature.

Serves 4 to 6

Garlic and Parmesan Grissini

3 cups (375 g/12 oz) plain (all-purpose) flour
1 tablespoon baking powder
1 teaspoon salt
1 cup (125 g/4 oz) grated Parmesan cheese
125 g (4 oz) butter, melted and cooled
1 large egg, beaten
3 cloves garlic, minced
½ cup (125 ml/4 fl oz) lukewarm water
sesame or poppy seeds (optional)
butter and flour for baking tray

1 Preheat oven to 190°C (375°F).
2 This step may be done in a processor. Sift the flour, baking powder and salt into a bowl, then stir in Parmesan. Make a well in the centre and add butter, egg, garlic and water. Stir until just mixed, then turn out onto a board and knead lightly for 5 minutes incorporating more flour if necessary to keep dough dry. Cover and refrigerate 30 minutes.
3 On a floured surface, roll out dough evenly to a rectangle about 25 x 30 cm (10 x 12 in) and ¾ cm (½ in) thick. Using a pastry wheel or long knife, cut into strips ¾ cm (½ in) wide, and of desired length.

If using sesame or poppy seeds, lightly roll bread sticks in these.
4 Butter and flour a baking tray, then arrange breadsticks 2 cm (¾ in) apart. Bake for 15 to 20 minutes, or until golden. For a softer dough, reduce oven temperature to 170°C (340°F) after the first 5 minutes.

Makes about 50 x 12 cm (5 in) sticks

STORING GRISSINI

When stored in an airtight jar, these breadsticks keep crisp for weeks. They may be baked for less time to give a softer, more breadlike texture, in which case they do not keep as well. They can be cut into short lengths to be served as snacks, or longer sticks to serve at table.

SOUPS & SALADS

THE ITALIANS TRULY HAVE A SOUP FOR EVERY SEASON. MANY ARE FULL-BODIED MEALS IN THEMSELVES, BEING BASED ON RICE, POTATOES, PASTA OR BREAD.

The Tuscans, in particular, sometimes use bread as a basis for soup, while in the Veneto the most common soup, *pasta e fagioli*, is based on borlotti beans which were originally from Mexico. On the coast fish soups are very popular. In Trieste soup often contains rice with eggs and lemon juice, like the Greek *avgolemono* and in Calabria, soup is fundamental to the relatively simple diet. Remember the importance of a flavourful garnish — add fresh basil, finely chopped fennel, marjoram, or a flourish of freshly grated Parmesan cheese to bring out the flavour!

A leafy salad, soup and bread constitute the light, fresh Italian style of eating. Many Italian salads are very beautiful to look at, as well as being delicious. It is to their cuisine we owe the discovery of delicious and colourful salad tidbits, such as baby artichokes and olives — all dressed, of course, with the finest quality olive oil, balsamic wine vinegar and fresh herbs.

Remember always that what is most important when preparing a salad is the freshness of the ingredients.

Zuppa di Cozze

1 kg (2 lb) fresh mussels
handful plain flour
2 tablespoons olive oil
40 g (1½ oz) butter
1 leek, white part only, finely chopped
3 cloves garlic, minced
pinch saffron flakes or powder
1 tablespoon finely chopped
coriander or parsley
1 small red chilli, minced
⅔ cup (150 ml/5 fl oz) dry
white wine
200 g (6½ oz) fresh tomatoes, peeled,
seeded and chopped
1 cup (250 ml/8 fl oz) water
salt

1 Put mussels in a bowl, sprinkle with flour and cover with cold water. Leave for 15 minutes then drain, scrub and debeard them, discarding any which are open.

2 Heat oil and butter in a large saucepan and sauté leek and garlic over a low heat until leeks are softened but not brown. Add saffron, coriander and chilli and cook, stirring, 1 to 2 minutes. Increase heat and add wine. Bring to the boil and allow to bubble for 1 to 2 minutes, then add tomatoes and water. Simmer with the lid on for 20 minutes. Check consistency here; it may be necessary to increase heat and boil to thicken slightly.

3 Add mussels to pan and cook, covered, until they are opened. Discard any which are now unopened, and throw away the shells of one-third of the remaining so that the soup is not crowded with shells. Season to taste. Serve immediately with crusty bread.

Serves 6

MUSSEL SOUP

Mussels seem to be at their best in soup. In *Zuppa di Cozze* they contrast well with the subtle flavour of the broth and there is great eye appeal as well.

MUSSELS

Mussels are delicious and readily obtainable along the Italian coast. Certain species are to be found in inland lakes and rivers, too, but it is those mussels which are fished from the sea which are thought to have the best flavour. If you have never experimented with buying and cooking mussels, you will discover that there is a great variety of types and sizes. Some are no larger than your little fingernail, others can exceed 12 cm (4½ in) in length. Some delicatessens sell preserved mussels in herbed vinegar, which can be a tasty addition to an antipasto platter.

Prior to preparing the dish of your choice, place the mussels in a bucket of fresh water for 20 minutes; discard any which float or have opened, or which have broken shells. Place the mussels into another bucket, cover with water and sprinkle with salt. Leave for a further hour to 90 minutes before checking for any additional ones which may have opened. These should also be discarded. Finally, rinse mussels under cold running water to clean thoroughly.

Roasted Asparagus with Fontina

225 g (7 oz) Fontina cheese, cut into small dice
milk
30 g (1 oz) butter
2 egg yolks, beaten
salt and white pepper
1 kg (2 lb) fresh asparagus, trimmed and peeled
2 tablespoons olive oil
Parmesan cheese, grated

1 Put Fontina in a bowl and pour in enough milk to just cover. Set aside for at least 4 hours to allow the cheese to absorb the milk.
2 Preheat oven to 260°C (500°F).
3 Gently melt butter in the top of a double saucepan. Maintain a hot temperature, but do not allow water to boil. Add the cheese and any remaining milk, and stir in the egg yolks. Cook gently, stirring, until the mixture is thick and creamy. Season with salt and pepper and keep warm.
4 Place asparagus on a baking tray and pour over the olive oil. Toss with your fingers to coat them well, then space them over the tray so that they do not touch. Place in the oven and roast for 7 to 10 minutes, depending on thickness.

5 Arrange asparagus on warmed plates and spoon the sauce, known as *fondata* over the top. Serve at once with grated Parmesan cheese.

Serves 4 to 6

FONTINA

Fontina is the famous melting cheese from Piedmont which goes into *fondata,* the creamy Italian version of fondue. Used in a sauce for asparagus it makes an elegant but rich first course. It is not necessary to buy imported Italian Fontina as that made elsewhere will be just as successful in this recipe.

Potato, Onion and Zucchini Soup

1 tablespoon olive oil
30 g (1 oz) butter
450 g (14 oz) mild onions
or leeks, sliced
2 zucchini (courgettes), sliced
450 g (14 oz) potatoes, diced
8 cups (2 litres/64 fl oz) water
pinch chilli flakes
salt

1 Melt oil and butter in a large, heavy-based saucepan and add onions. Sauté over a low heat until soft. Add zucchini, toss to coat, then sauté 1 to 2 minutes. Add potatoes and water and simmer over a low heat until potatoes are cooked and start to break down. If necessary, increase heat to thicken, or add some more water to thin. Towards the end of cooking add chilli flakes.

2 Force mixture through a sieve, or process in a mouli. If using a blender or processor, go easy as the ideal texture is coarse with little pieces of zucchini visible. Season with salt to taste before serving.

Serves 4 to 6

POTATO, ONION AND ZUCCHINI SOUP

Based on *licurdia,* a soup from Cosenza in Calabria, this version is simple, flavoursome and attractive. It makes a good first course before a roast or lasagne, and is equally delicious when served lightly chilled on a hot summer's day.

Tuna and White Bean Salad

1 clove garlic, minced
1 teaspoon finely chopped fresh thyme, or ¼ teaspoon dried
1 tablespoon finely chopped fresh parsley
3 tablespoons white wine vinegar
4 tablespoons extra virgin olive oil
salt and freshly ground black pepper
600 g (1 lb 3 oz) cooked cannellini beans
1 large red onion, coarsely chopped
750 g (1½ lb) canned tuna in oil, drained and broken up into chunks
3 hard-boiled eggs, sliced into wedges
3 tomatoes, sliced into wedges

1 Combine garlic, thyme, parsley, vinegar and olive oil and mix with a fork until blended. Season with salt and pepper.
2 Place beans and onion into a large bowl, add dressing and toss to coat well. Add tuna, toss gently, then add half the egg wedges and half the tomato. Lightly combine. Serve piled onto a platter with the remaining egg and tomato wedges for garnish.

Serves 4 to 6

CANNELLINI BEANS

Using canned ready-cooked cannellini beans is convenient but as with all dried beans, boiling them yourself gives a better texture and is more economical. Remember, dried beans which are old do not cook properly.

Cover beans well with cold water and leave to soak overnight in a warm spot. This step is necessary to prevent the skins from splitting. Then drain them, cover with fresh cold water and bring to the boil. Simmer for 2 hours, only salting at the end.

Fresh Figs with Prosciutto

**3 tablespoons freshly grated
Parmesan cheese**
1 tablespoon finely grated lemon zest
125 g (4 oz) butter
4 thin slices prosciutto, cut in half
8 fresh, ripe figs

1 Combine Parmesan and lemon
zest and set aside.
2 Melt butter in a saucepan and
bring to bubbling over a moderate
heat. Continue simmering until it
clarifies (the fats separate) and the
colour turns golden brown. Strain,
and keep warm.
3 Wrap a strip of prosciutto around
the middle of each fig. Place on a
rack well below a hot grill and heat
through, about 2 minutes. Arrange
2 per serve on warmed plates, spoon
over some browned butter and
sprinkle some of the Parmesan mix
on top. Serve immediately,
accompanied by the rest of the
Parmesan mix.

Serves 4

FIGS

Figs are one of the oldest of fruits, and have been
cultivated since very early times. Indeed, some
sources assure us that the fruit Eve plucked in the
Garden of Eden was a fig, and not an apple. Figs
were also grown in the Hanging Gardens of Babylon
and were a favourite food of the ancient Greeks and
Romans. Figs are truly a taste of paradise, Italian-
style. Their flavour and aroma conjure up images of
summer and bestow a relaxed languor upon the
person fortunate enough to be eating them.
Prosciutto is an uncooked, unsmoked ham which has
been salted and air-cured. It is sometimes called
Parma ham, although not all prosciutto is necessarily
from there. It is sweet and succulent and, together
with the luscious figs, creates a lush and colourful
dish that tastes absolutely delicious — it is especially
nice when eaten out of doors on a warm evening!

PASTA

PASTA ... ITS FORM, INGREDIENTS AND USES VARY GREATLY THROUGHOUT ITALY. FOR INSTANCE, UNIQUE TO ABRUZZI, A MOUNTAINOUS REGION ON THE ADRIATIC COAST, IS THE CHITARRA, A WOODEN FRAME ROUGHLY IN THE SHAPE OF A GUITAR, STRUNG ON EACH SIDE WITH WIRE. PASTA DOUGH IS ROLLED OVER THE WIRE, WHICH CUTS IT INTO STRIPS SIMILAR TO LINGUINE.

Pasta from Abruzzi has an excellent reputation, said to be because of the quality of the local water used in the making. A good number of the pasta shapes common today began in Apulia, which has bumper crops of durum wheat. Apulians are Italy's prima pasta eaters, but due to the lack of eggs in the region in the past, their home-made pasta is often still egg-less.

The Italians have developed a myriad of sauces to accompany their pasta dishes, many now world-famed, such as the redoubtable *pesto*. Although often originated for pasta, this endlessly diverse variety of sauces is just as likely to be used today to dress vegetables and salads, or to be tossed through stir-fried meats.

You will find an enormous variety of pasta on offer at your food store. Many imported and local brands of dried pasta serve very well; however, for certain dishes such as these described here, it is worth seeking out an exceptional brand of fresh pasta or even making your own.

Taglierini with Salmon, Peas and Lemon

250 g (8 oz) shelled young peas
salt
400 g (13 oz) fresh taglierini or 250 g (8 oz) dried
90 g (3 oz) butter
1 tablespoon vegetable oil
1 clove garlic
350 g (11 oz) fresh salmon, skinned, boned and cut into 2 cm (¾ in) cubes
3 tablespoons finely chopped fresh parsley
freshly ground black pepper
¼ teaspoon grated lemon zest
1 teaspoon fresh lemon juice

1 Bring a large saucepan of water to the boil, add peas and a pinch of salt and simmer until *al dente*. Scoop from water and reserve. Add pasta to the pot and cook until *al dente*.
2 In the meantime, heat butter and oil in a frying pan and briefly sauté garlic clove. Add salmon with a pinch of salt and sauté gently until opaque, but not browned. Add peas and parsley to pan and cook, stirring, for 1 minute. Discard garlic. Season with pepper and stir in lemon zest and juice.
3 When pasta is ready, drain and add to sauce. Toss lightly to coat and serve at once.

Serves 4

Linguine with Beetroot

250 g (8 oz) beetroot, cooked
40 g (1½ oz) butter
1 tablespoon finely chopped onion
2 sprigs fresh thyme
salt and freshly ground black pepper
3 tablespoons dry white wine
⅔ cup (150 ml/5 fl oz) cream
2 egg yolks, lightly beaten
350 g (11 oz) fresh linguine or 250 g (8 oz) dried

1 Cut one-third of the beetroot into julienne strips and reserve for garnish. Cut the remaining two-thirds into larger pieces.
2 Heat butter in a large pan and add pieces of beetroot, onion and 1 sprig thyme. Sauté gently 2 to 3 minutes, season lightly with salt and pepper and pour in wine. Cook, stirring, over a high heat to reduce wine. When the mixture is almost dry, transfer to a processor and blend until smooth. Return to pan and keep warm.
3 Whip cream until thick, then stir in egg yolks. Gradually add to beetroot in pan and bring to the boil, stirring. Taste for salt and pepper.
4 In the meantime, cook pasta in boiling salted water until *al dente*. Drain, add to sauce and toss. Transfer to warmed pasta bowls, decorate with reserved beetroot and sprinkle over remaining thyme leaves.

Serves 4

Spaghetti and Prawns in Lemon Sauce

500 g (1 lb) fresh spaghetti, or 300 g (10 oz) dried
1 cup (250 ml/8 fl oz) cream
½ teaspoon grated lemon zest
3 tablespoons grappa
1 tablespoon fresh lemon juice
pinch nutmeg
450 g (14 oz) cooked and peeled prawns (shrimps)

1 Put spaghetti on to boil in a large pot of boiling, salted water. Just before it becomes *al dente*, drain.
2 Meanwhile, put cream and lemon zest in a frying pan and simmer over a low heat for 5 minutes. Add grappa, lemon juice and nutmeg, cook 1 to 2 minutes, then stir in prawns. Add drained spaghetti, increase heat and cook, stirring, so that the sauce thickens and becomes absorbed by the pasta. Serve at once, without cheese.

Serves 4

SPAGHETTI AND PRAWNS IN LEMON SAUCE

This is a combination of two dishes: a delicate prawn pasta from the Ligurian coast and a creamy lemon sauce flavoured with grappa from the mountains beyond. If grappa is unavailable or too powerful for you, vodka is a milder substitute.

Hazelnut and Ricotta Agnolotti

PASTA
3¼ cups (400 g/13 oz) plain (all-purpose) flour
large pinch salt
4 eggs
FILLING
⅔ cup (100 g/3½ oz) roasted and peeled hazelnuts (filberts)
100 g (3½ oz) Ricotta cheese
½ cup (60 g/2 oz) grated Parmesan cheese
yolk of 1 large egg
good pinch nutmeg
pinch salt
1 to 2 tablespoons milk
1 egg white, beaten
SAUCE
90 g (3 oz) butter
4 tablespoons cream
5 to 6 small fresh sage leaves
2 tablespoons freshly grated Parmesan cheese

1 To prepare pasta: Pile flour on a work surface, make a well in the centre and add salt and eggs. Using a fork, break up eggs and begin to incorporate the flour. Continue blending until you have a loosely formed mass of dough. The dough may be made in a processor up to this point.

Begin kneading by hand, adding a little more flour or water as needed. Continue kneading until a smooth elastic ball is formed. Cover with a damp cloth or plastic wrap and rest for 30 minutes. Divide the ball into four, then using a rolling pin or a hand-cranked pasta machine, roll out each in turn to a very thin, even sheet. Rest, covered.

2 To prepare filling: Crush hazelnuts in a mortar or use a rolling pin over a hard surface. Avoid processing, as this tends to purée the nuts. In a bowl combine them with ricotta, Parmesan, nutmeg and salt. Stir in just enough milk to form a paste.

3 Using a cookie cutter or an upturned glass, cut out circles from the sheets of pasta about 5 cm (2 in) in diameter. Keep all the pasta covered as you work to avoid drying out. Working on a few at a time, paint around the rim of each circle with egg white. Place a little of the filling in the centre of each, then fold it over to form a half moon shape. Firmly press the edges together then cut around them with a zig-zag pastry wheel. As the agnolotti are formed, place them in a single layer and dust very lightly with flour.

4 When they are all made, simmer in boiling salted water until *al dente*, 3 to 4 minutes.

5 To prepare sauce: Melt butter in a saucepan and cook over a low heat until browned. Strain into another pan and add cream and sage. Heat gently to thicken slightly, then stir in Parmesan. Keep warm.

6 Drain agnolotti, transfer to a warmed serving dish and toss through the sauce. Serve at once, accompanied with extra grated Parmesan.

Serves 4

FRESH PASTA

Fresh pasta (Pasta fresca) is available from specialty pasta shops and delicatessens and in the refrigerator in supermarkets. It is often displayed in bulk and you can purchase as little or as much as you need. This pasta is quite pliable and takes a very short time to cook (1½ to 3 minutes). The key point to look for? Fresh pasta should be light and tender, never sticky or heavy feeling.

A tip to remember: the success of a pasta dish depends on the correct proportion of water to pasta. Use a minimum of 3 litres (5 pints) water for every 375 g (12 oz) pasta. Too little water and the pasta will be crowded and unable to cook evenly; it will go gluey as the relatively small amount of water becomes starch-laden.

SUN-DRIED TOMATOES

Sun-dried tomatoes (Pomodori secchi) are available in the dry state or marinated in oil, often with garlic and herbs. They can be dark and concentrated in flavour, or lighter and plumper, with a more subtle taste. These delicious tid-bits may stand alone on an antipasto platter on their own merits, perhaps with a few pickled vegetables or pieces of fresh mozzarella, or be included as part of a 'finger food' recipe. Theirs is the quintessential taste of summer.

Preferably, buy those sun-dried tomatoes which have been packed in the best quality extra virgin olive oil you can afford. The air-dried ones which are sold in supermarkets are usually all seeds and do not reconstitute successfully in cooking.

Or, it is an easy matter to make your own sun-dried tomatoes. Cut the tomatoes in halves or quarters and place them, cut side up on a baking sheet. Sprinkle lightly with salt and bake in a very slow oven for up to 7 hours. Then pack them in clean glass jars in layers, interleaving them with sprinklings of fresh chopped herbs and whole garlic cloves. Then cover with extra-virgin olive oil and cap securely; refrigerate after opening.

Pappardelle with Sun-Dried Tomatoes

½ red capsicum (pepper)
½ yellow capsicum (pepper)
3 tablespoons olive oil
3 spring onions, sliced
60 g (2 oz) ham, thickly sliced
1 small fresh red chilli, finely chopped
5 pieces sun-dried tomatoes in oil, drained and sliced
2 tablespoons extra virgin olive oil
freshly ground black pepper
600 g (1 lb 3 oz) fresh pappardelle or 400 g (13 oz) dried
1 tablespoon shredded fresh basil

1 Place capsicums under a hot grill and roast until skin is blackened and blistered. When cooled, peel off skins, wipe clean and cut into strips.
2 Heat oil in a large frying pan and add onions, ham and chilli. Sauté briefly, then add dried tomatoes, oil and roasted peppers. Toss until heated through then season with pepper.
3 In the meantime, cook pappardelle in boiling salted water until *al dente*. Drain. Transfer to pan with sauce, add basil and toss lightly to combine. Divide between warmed pasta bowls and serve at once, accompanied by freshly grated Parmesan cheese.

Serves 4

Tortellini with Pistachios and Basil

600 g (1 lb 3 oz) cheese-filled tortellini
90 g (3 oz) butter
60 g (2 oz) shelled pistachio kernels, crushed
4 to 6 tablespoons cream
1 tablespoon finely chopped fresh basil
freshly ground Parmesan cheese
freshly ground black pepper

1 Put the tortellini on to cook in boiling salted water.
2 In the meantime, melt butter in a frying pan or wok and when it starts to turn golden, stir in crushed pistachios. Cook over a low heat, stirring, 1 minute. Add 4 tablespoons cream and basil, and a few good grates of Parmesan. Taste for pepper. If the sauce becomes too thick, add more cream.
3 When tortellini is *al dente*, drain and add to frying pan. Toss to coat well, then transfer to warmed serving plates and serve at once. Pass around the Parmesan and pepper mill.

Serves 4

DELICIOUS BASIL

In so many ways, basil seems to be at the heart of Italian cookery. With the possible exception of marjoram, no other herb is used so widely. Basil may be used to flavour a wide variety of vegetable dishes, notably artichokes and zucchini, as well as the pasta dish described here. Its intense fragrance and aroma marry superbly with tomatoes, eggplant and mushrooms — all of which are indispensable in Italian cooking.

A tip to remember: fresh basil will bruise and blacken easily, even just in transit from the greengrocer's to your home. It is a simple matter to grow basil in a pot on a sunny balcony or windowsill; it thrives on being pinched back and will provide you with plenty of fresh flavour.

LIGHT MEALS

ITALIANS ARE GREAT EATERS, WHETHER AT HOME, IN ANTIPASTO BARS, *TRATTORIAS,* OR *RISTORANTES.* EATING IS REGARDED AS AN OPPORTUNITY FOR A CONGENIAL GET-TOGETHER OF FAMILY AND FRIENDS SO IT IS CALLED *IL CULTO DEL BEN ESSERE* — THE PURSUIT OF THE GOOD LIFE!

For this reason, the Italians' love of antipasto-style eating takes centre stage with these simple and elegant light main meals. Here we take a fresh look at some of the classic ingredients of Italian cuisine — tuna, olives, asparagus, artichokes and, naturally, pasta — in an imaginative way.

Ease of preparation characterises these recipes, and they all have a sure, light touch. All may be either presented as main meals, or served in slices or individual portions for a more informal occasion. The Italians are far too fresh and lively in their approach to life to be constrained when it comes to cookery!

In fact, this is what antipasto-style food is all about in today's kitchen: a filling meal ready in the time it takes to cook the tuna steak or the penne, and one which you can prepare yourself, easily and without fuss. The cooking time is brief, so the nutritional content of the ingredients is not lost — and there is the added bonus that often there is very little washing up.

Tonnato alla Genovese

3 tablespoons extra virgin olive oil
2 onions, sliced thinly
2 cloves garlic, finely chopped
200 g (6½ oz) Ligurian, Riviera or
Niçoise olives, pitted
1 tablespoon white wine vinegar
1 tablespoon fresh chopped, or 1
teaspoon dried marjoram
salt and freshly ground black pepper
1 teaspoon olive oil, extra
4 tuna steaks, about 3 cm
(1½ in) thick
1 tablespoon chopped fresh basil
and parsley combined

1 Preheat oven to 180°C (350°F).
2 Heat 3 tablespoons oil in a large frying pan. Add onions and garlic and cook gently for 10 minutes, stirring often. Add olives, vinegar, marjoram and salt and pepper to taste and cook a further 2 to 3 minutes.
3 Grease a baking dish with 1 teaspoon of oil, and arrange tuna steaks in a single layer across bottom. Lightly salt and pepper them before spooning over the onion olive sauce. Cover with foil and bake 15 minutes, or until tuna is just cooked through. Transfer to a warm serving plate, spoon the sauce over and sprinkle with basil and parsley.

Serves 4

BAKED TUNA
WITH OLIVES AND HERBS

This dish, *Tonnato alla Genovese*, uses ingredients which are all typical of Liguria. The local olives are small and firm fleshed and go well with the flavour of fresh tuna. Marjoram and basil are both used extensively in the region; in fact, if a recipe is 'alla Genovese' it invariably means with marjoram or with basil.

OLIVE OIL

Olive oil is probably the most important ingredient mentioned in any Italian recipe. Extra-virgin olive oil is made from the first pressing of slightly under-ripe olives, and the better brands are produced without chemical means. It has a low acidity (under 1 per cent, by law) and no cholesterol.

Always seek out and buy the very best quality, extra-virgin olive oil you can afford. It really does make a difference to the taste and texture of food. A good olive oil will enhance the flavours of delicate vegetables, such as asparagus, mushrooms and artichokes, while a heavier one will overwhelm them.

The flavour of olive oil can differ dramatically, depending upon the manufacturing process and where the olives came from. Some varieties have quite a nutty taste, others are peppery and still others have a fruity flavour and aroma. There is no 'right' flavour and fragrance — only the one which is right for you. Spend some time testing and tasting the different varieties of olive oil available until you find one that you particularly like.

Penne Mare e Monte

40 g (1½ oz) butter
¼ cup (30 g/1½ oz) plain (all-purpose) flour
2 cups (500 ml/16 fl oz) milk
1 bay leaf
pinch nutmeg
salt and freshly ground black pepper
1 tablespoon fresh lemon juice
500 g (1 lb) penne
4 tablespoons extra virgin olive oil
2 leeks, trimmed and thinly sliced
1 thin zucchini (courgette), sliced in julienne strips
500 g (1 lb) button mushrooms, sliced
½ cup (125 ml/4 fl oz) dry white wine
salt and freshly ground black pepper
300 g (10 oz) canned tuna in oil, drained

1 Preheat oven to 200°C (400°F). Grease a shallow-sided ovenproof dish.
2 To prepare sauce: Melt butter in a saucepan and stir in flour. Cook until bubbling then gradually stir in milk. Add bay leaf and cook over a moderate heat, stirring often, until thickened. Season with nutmeg, salt and pepper and stir in lemon juice. Remove from heat and set aside.
3 Cook penne in plenty of boiling salted water until *al dente*. Drain and stir through 1 tablespoon of the oil.

4 Heat remaining oil in a pan and gently sauté leeks until softened. Add zucchini and mushrooms, sauté 1 minute then add wine. Cook over high heat for 10 to 15 seconds then season to taste with salt and pepper and sauté 1 minute more. Remove bay leaf from sauce and then add three-quarters of sauce and the penne to pan. Toss to combine and transfer to prepared dish.
5 Break the tuna up and distribute throughout the penne. Spoon over remaining sauce. Transfer to oven and bake until hot, about 20 minutes. Serve at once.

Serves 6

PENNE OF THE SEA AND THE MOUNTAINS

Penne Mare e Monte — an appealing baked pasta dish using tuna (from the sea) and mushrooms (from the mountains). This can be prepared in advance and popped in the oven just before serving. Use imported tuna from Italy if possible.

49

Polenta Pasticciata

40 g (1½ oz) butter
2 tablespoons plain (all-purpose) flour
1¾ cups (420 ml/14 fl oz) milk
salt and white pepper
pinch nutmeg
90 g (3 oz) grated cheese, such as
Cheddar, Emmenthal or Fontina
4 cups (1 litre/32 fl oz) water
½ teaspoon salt
220 g (7 oz) polenta
100 g (3½ oz) butter, cut into pieces
300 g (10 oz) button mushrooms,
sliced
salt and freshly ground black pepper
pinch nutmeg
480 g (15 oz) drained artichoke
hearts, sliced
3 tomatoes, sliced
180 g (6 oz) double smoked ham,
thinly sliced
2 tablespoons grated
Parmesan cheese

1 Preheat oven to 200°C (400°F). Oil an ovenproof dish.
2 To prepare sauce: Melt butter in a saucepan and stir in flour. Cook briefly, then gradually blend in milk. Stir until thickened. Season with salt and pepper to taste, and nutmeg. Add cheese. Cook, stirring, until sauce is smooth.
3 Boil water in a large saucepan. Add salt and gradually stir in polenta. Reduce heat and cook, stirring often, for 20 minutes. Remove from heat and stir in half the butter.
4 Meanwhile, melt remaining butter and gently sauté mushrooms for 3 to 4 minutes. Season with salt, pepper and nutmeg.
5 Spread one-third of polenta into prepared dish and top with one-third mushrooms. Then one-third artichoke hearts, one-third tomato slices, one-third ham, and one-third sauce. Repeat these layers twice. Sprinkle with Parmesan and bake for 30 minutes. Stand for 3 to 4 minutes before serving.

Serves 4

POLENTA PASTICCIATA

Sometimes called *pastissada*, versions of this pie of filled and baked polenta can be found all over northern Italy. Every town, every cook has their special recipe which is of course *supremo*, but this one is hard to beat.

Torta Pasquale

Savoury Easter pies are common to most of Italy, and although there are many variations they are all meatless or di magro, *literally meaning lean.*

500 g (1 lb) puff pastry
750 g (1½ lb) pre-cooked spinach,
squeezed dry and chopped
large pinch nutmeg
¼ teaspoon salt
2 tablespoons grated Parmesan cheese
freshly ground black pepper
2 eggs, beaten
300 g (10 oz) artichoke hearts, sliced
into 5 along their lengths
3 hard-boiled eggs, each cut into
5 to 6 slices
2 tablespoons pine nuts

1 Preheat oven to 200°C (400°F) and grease a 21 cm (8 in) springform pan.
2 Divide puff pastry in two, roughly two-thirds and one-third of whole. Roll out the larger piece, then line prepared pan, bringing it 5 to 6 cm (about 2 in) up the sides.
3 In a bowl mix spinach, nutmeg, salt, Parmesan and pepper to taste. Add three-quarters of the beaten eggs and combine well. Reserve remaining egg for glazing.

4 Layer one-third of the spinach in pie base and cover with the artichoke slices in a single layer. Put another one-third of spinach on this, then cover with the egg slices. Layer the remaining spinach on top.
5 Roll out remaining pastry and place over the pie. Press top and bottom edges tightly and pinch the two together. Trim edges before painting the surface with reserved egg. Make one or two small cuts in the pastry, then sprinkle the pine nuts on top. Place in the oven and bake until pastry is golden, about 45 minutes. Allow to cool slightly before removing from pan. Can be served warm or cold.

TORTA PASQUALE

In Liguria where this recipe is from, spinach is frequently used and spring artichokes are in good supply. In other regions a Torta Pasquale will often contain Ricotta but this cheese was not commonly used in traditional Ligurian kitchens until quite recently. Whole or sliced eggs are baked into the pie and this signifies the ever regenerating elements of nature after the passing of winter.

Asparagus Frittata

6 eggs
¼ cup (60 ml/2 fl oz) cream
1 tablespoon plain (all-purpose) flour
pinch nutmeg
3 tablespoons grated Parmesan cheese
salt and white pepper
400 g (13 oz) cooked green asparagus spears, either canned or fresh
1 tablespoon finely diced spring onion
2 tablespoons olive oil

1 In a bowl whisk eggs, cream, flour, nutmeg, Parmesan, and salt and pepper to taste.
2 Cut half the asparagus spears into 2 cm (¾ in) lengths and add to custard along with the spring onion.
3 Heat oil in a large heavy-based frying pan. Add custard and arrange remaining asparagus spears in a spoke-like pattern around the surface. Cover pan, turn heat down to very low and cook until the frittata is set, about 20 minutes. Serve warm.

Serves 6 to 8

The asparagus is a member of the lily family. It is simple to prepare, delicious to eat and, as a bonus, turns a fabulous, intensely bright green on being cooked.

Considering how easy it is to grow, it is surprising that asparagus is not seen more often in our kitchens. It does best in mild to cool climates. If you are buying your asparagus, look for stalks that are bright green, crisp and firm, topped by leaf buds that are tightly closed and mauve-green in colour. Avoid any produce that looks withered. Trim off the woody ends before use, and use a vegetable peeler to scrape stalks to about halfway up. A good tip to remember if preparing asparagus ahead of time is to sprinkle the stalks with a splash of lemon juice or mild-flavoured vinegar. This will stop them from becoming discoloured.

INDEX